CONTENTS

Blast off!

We have explored much of our world, but most of space remains unexplored by us. All kinds of machines and craft travel there. Some help us to understand the mysteries of the Universe. Others give us satellite TV!

On the launch pad
Rockets are known as **launch vehicles**. They are the biggest, fastest, noisiest moving machines ever made. They burn tonnes of fuel each second as they lift all kinds of **payloads** into space, from **satellites** to **space stations**.

Round and round

Satellites orbit the Earth, the Moon, and other planets such as Mars and Saturn. They are like our space servants, doing their jobs by remote control as they whiz round and round in the cold, silent emptiness.

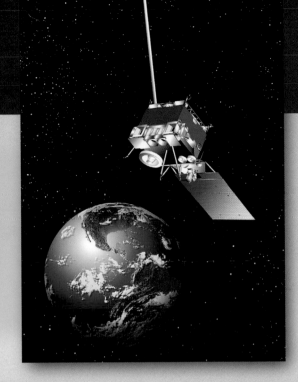

Floating free

Crafts and machines without people can do lots of tasks in space. But sometimes a human is needed, floating weightless yet safe in a spacesuit.

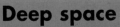

Deep space

Space **probes** fitted with cameras, detectors and sensors travel on vast, lonely trips to other planets. They send back faint **radio signals** to tell us what they see and find. Then they go deeper into never-ending space, on and on and on …

Launch rocket

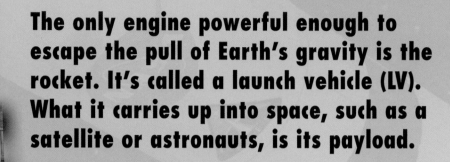

The only engine powerful enough to escape the pull of Earth's gravity is the rocket. It's called a launch vehicle (LV). What it carries up into space, such as a satellite or astronauts, is its payload.

Europe's *Ariane 5* is a 'heavy lifter', carrying many tonnes into orbit. In the main part of the rocket is a giant fuel tank, with the rocket engine at the bottom and the payload in the nose cone.

Massive **solid-fuel** rocket **boosters** give extra power after launch.

Stats and Facts

3 ... 2 ... 1 ... Ignition ... Lift-off! US Atlas rockets have launched more than 80 space missions. The fuel burns in a continuous explosion, thrusting the rocket skywards.

Ariane 5

Operator: European Space Agency (France)

Height: 59 metres

Width: 5.4 metres

Weight: 780 tonnes

Payload: 21 tonnes into Low Earth Orbit

First stage engine: 1 Vulcain, burn time 7 minutes

Boosters: Solid fuel, burn time 130 seconds

Second stage engine: 1 Aestus, burn time 18 minutes

THAT'S INCREDIBLE

To get away from Earth's **gravity** and reach space, a rocket must travel at speeds of at least 11,000 metres per second.

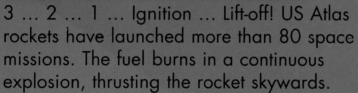

The boosters drop off after launch.

Space shuttle

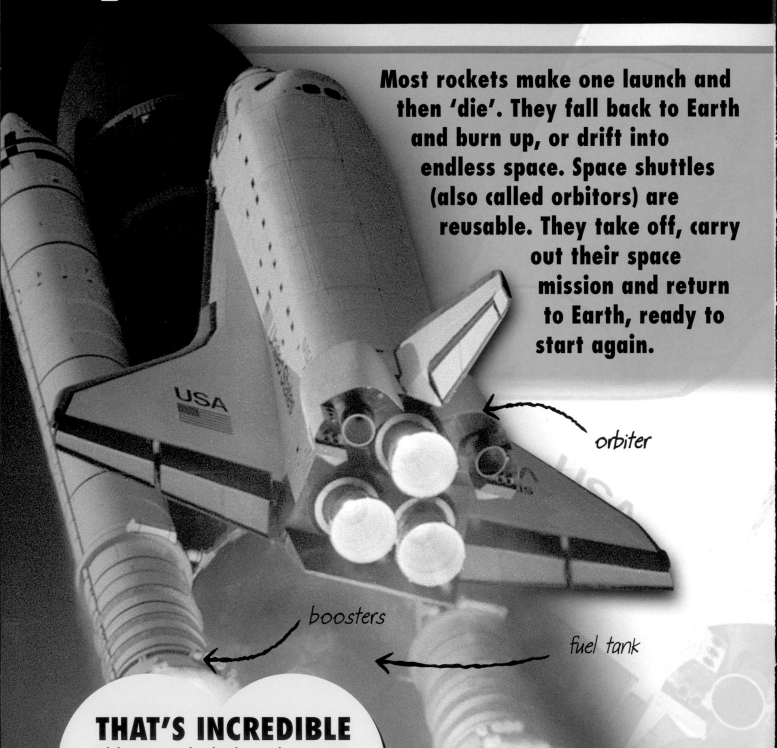

Most rockets make one launch and then 'die'. They fall back to Earth and burn up, or drift into endless space. Space shuttles (also called orbitors) are reusable. They take off, carry out their space mission and return to Earth, ready to start again.

orbiter

boosters

fuel tank

THAT'S INCREDIBLE
While in space, the shuttle travels at 27,800 kilometres per hour, which is almost eight kilometres every second!

The orbiter comes back to Earth and lands on a runway without engine power. It's the world's biggest glider, touching down at 350 kilometres per hour.

Space shuttle

Maker: NASA (USA)

Orbiter length: 37.2 metres

Orbiter wingspan: 23.8 metres

Orbiter height: 17.9 metres

Orbiter weight: 110 tonnes

Orbiter engines: 3 Rocketdynes

Booster height: 45.6 metres

Booster weight: 590 tonnes

Fuel tank height: 47 metres

Fuel tank weight: 750 tonnes

Complete take-off weight: 2,000-plus tonnes

This shuttle is carrying a satellite back to Earth for repairs.

The crew controls the orbiter using on-board computers. The computers also help them to carry out space missions.

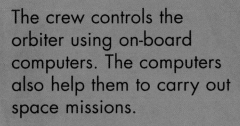

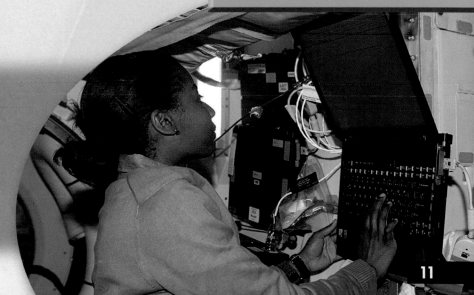

Satellites galore

Thousands of satellites orbit planet Earth. They do all kinds of jobs, from helping to forecast weather to mapping the land and sea, looking into deep space – and spying on possible enemies below.

Navstars send out radio signals with their position and time to **satnav** receivers.

solar panel

THAT'S INCREDIBLE
With the best decoder equipment, a satnav receiver can pinpoint its position to the nearest three metres!

Technicians prepare a satellite that will be used to make weather forecasts.

Navstar series

Purpose: Global Positioning System (GPS) satellites for navigation

Maker: Rockwell, Lockheed-Martin, Boeing North American (USA)

Width: Up to 11.4 metres including solar panels

Height: Up to 3.4 metres

Weight: Up to 2.2 tonnes

Power: Solar panels generate 1,000 watts (1 kW)

Launch vehicle: Delta

Orbital height: 20,200 km

Orbital speed: 3.8 metres per second

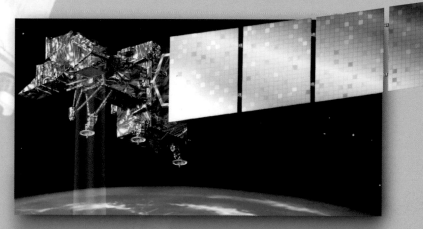

Landsats photograph Earth's surface for map-makers and surveyors. Their powerful cameras photograph overlapping areas of Earth to make up a complete view.

Spy satellites take photographs of buildings from space.

Comsats

Comsats are communications satellites. Without them we'd have no satellite television, no instant phone calls to anywhere in the world, and almost no computer Internet!

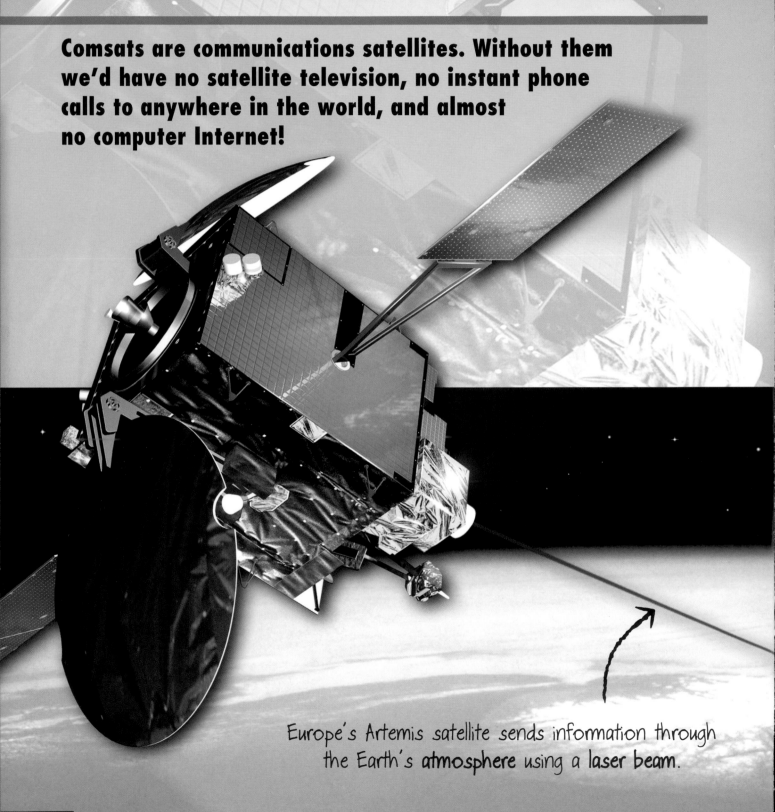

Europe's Artemis satellite sends information through the Earth's **atmosphere** using a laser beam.

THAT'S INCREDIBLE

About 10-20 **comsats** are launched every year. Their average cost is £40-£50 million each!

antennae

Comsats have several dish-like **antennae** (aerials). One receives signals to be broadcast from Earth. Another broadcasts signals back down to Earth.

Boeing 376 Comsat

Purpose: Satellite TV for UK and neighbouring countries

Maker and model: Hughes-Boeing HS-376 (USA)

Width: 2.2 metres

Height: 7.76 metres including antenna

Launch date: 19 December 2000

Launch vehicle: *Ariane 5*

Weight at launch: 1,420 kilograms

Weight in orbit: 824 kilograms

Orbital height: 35,800 kilometres

The Boeing 376 was the first comsat to be launched by the space shuttle.

Space telescope

telescope
cover door

mirror
compartment

instrument
compartment

Why send a telescope into space? High above the Earth's surface there are no clouds, no blurring caused by the atmosphere (the layer of air around Earth) and no interference from Earth's lights. It's a clear view, all day, every day.

The Hubble Space Telescope (HST) was launched from the space shuttle in 1990.

THAT'S INCREDIBLE

After Hubble's launch, its mirror was found to be 1/400th of a millimetre out of shape. A repair mission costing millions of dollars fixed the problem.

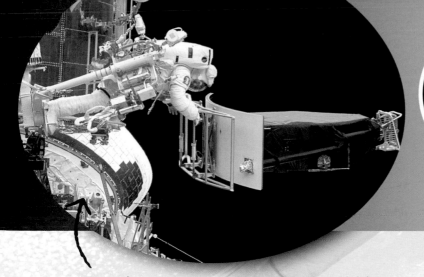

Hubble Space Telescope

Maker: NASA (USA)

Length: 13.1 metres

Width: 4.27 metres

Weight: 11.1 tonnes

Orbital height: Average 590 kilometres

Orbital speed: 7,500 metres per second

Orbital time: 97 minutes

Service missions: 1993 (repair mirror), 1997 (fit new instruments), 1999 (running repairs), 2002 (fit new camera)

Shuttle astronauts took the Hubble Telescope apart to fit a new, better mirror.

This beautiful shot of stars being formed was taken by the Hubble Telescope.

The James Webb Telescope will be launched around 2013. It will see to the edge of the Universe, and look for signs of life.

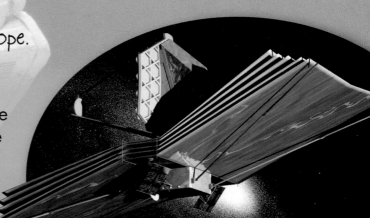

17

Space station

Space stations are built so people can live and work in space. They are built piece by piece. The parts are carried up by space shuttles and rockets. The latest space station is the International Space Station (ISS), which will be completed in 2010.

THAT'S INCREDIBLE

Russian astronaut Valeri Polyakov holds the record for living in space. In 1995 he stayed on board *Mir* for 438 days — well over a year!

The space shuttle orbiter *Atlantis* **docked** with the Russian space station *Mir* in 1995.

International Space Station (ISS)

Makers: Various

Length: 58 metres

Width: 73 metres, including solar panels

Height: 27 metres

Weight: 470 tonnes when complete

Orbital height: 340 kilometres

Orbits per 24 hours: Almost 16

First crew: Went aboard in 2000

Call sign: Alpha

Completion due: 2010

The first space station was the US Skylab in 1973, but one of the solar panels fell off at its launch.

solar panel

Space tourists journey to the ISS at a cost of £13 million each.

Space shuttle orbiters deliver new parts to the ISS.

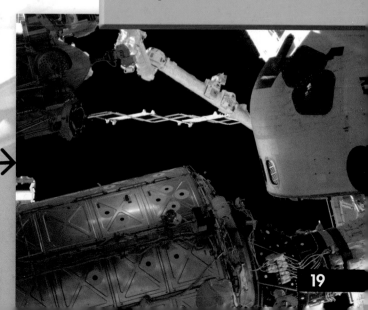

Spacesuits

In space there is no air to breathe, and it's freezing cold out of the Sun and boiling hot in it. A spacesuit keeps its astronaut alive and comfortable, for work outside the spacecraft.

THAT'S INCREDIBLE

In a spacesuit, the innermost layer is the MAG, Maximum Absorption Garment. It's like a soft nappy to soak up the astronaut's urine.

This astronaut is strapped into the Manned Manoeuvring Unit (MMU). It is like an armchair with tiny rocket thrusters.

A spacesuit has tubes that provide air and cooling water, and has a microphone and headphones in the helmet.

Canadarm2 robot arm

headlights and video camera

safety harness frame

tether straps

EMU Spacesuit

Makers: Various

Suit weight: 127 kilograms on Earth, nothing in space

Suit cover thickness: 5 millimetres

Number of layers: 13 including outer cover (1 layer), thermal garment (8 layers), pressure garment (2 layers), cooled undergarment (2 layers)

Undergarment: Temperature controlled by cooled water through 100 metres of tubing

Wearing time: Up to 7 hours

Cost: £6 million per suit

Astronauts in the ISS (see pages 18-19) use spacesuits when working outside. Tether straps stop them from floating away into space.

The Red Planet

The planet visited most by spacecraft is Mars. It looks red because its rocks and dust contain iron oxide – rust! About 40 missions have set off to Mars, but over half have failed to get there.

THAT'S INCREDIBLE

Mars **rovers** *Spirit* and *Opportunity* were named by a nine-year-old girl, Sufi Collies, who won a poetry competition.

Mars Express went into orbit around the planet on Christmas Day, 2003. It has taken thousands of detailed pictures of the mountains, valleys, dust plains and weather.

Stats and Facts

Spirit and **Opportunity** twin Mars rovers

Mission: Mars Exploration Rover

Landing date: January 2004

Length: 1.6 metres

Width: 2.3 metres

Height: 1.5 metres

Weight: 180 kilograms

Power: Solar panels generate 140 watts

Top speed: 5 centimetres per second

Average speed: 1 centimetre per second

Drive: 6 electric motors, each turning a 25-centimetre diameter wheel

Two Viking craft landed on Mars in 1976, and took pictures like this.

Two rovers, Spirit (left) and Opportunity, landed there 28 years later.

Moon landing

Between 1969 and 1972, twelve US astronauts walked on the Moon. They are the only people ever to have set foot on another world.

The rocket *Saturn V* blasted off on 16th July 1969, carrying the spacecraft *Apollo 11*. The journey to the Moon took four days.

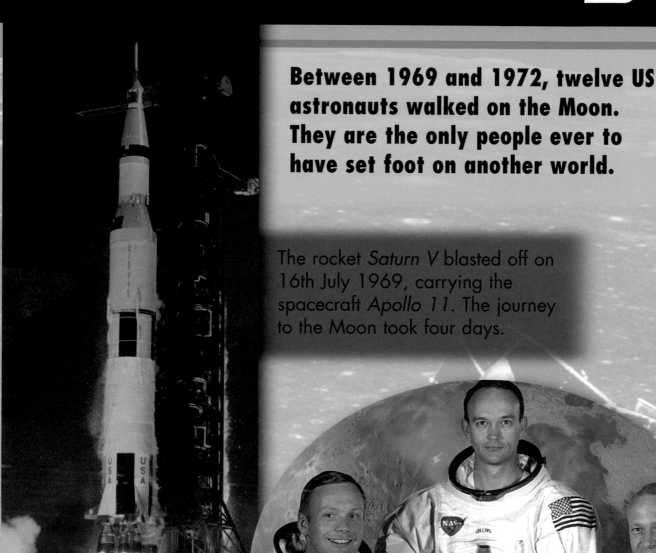

First to set foot on the Moon was Neil Armstrong (centre right). He climbed down to the dusty surface, saying: "That's one small step for a man, one giant leap for mankind."

Stats and Facts

Apollo Lunar Module Lander

Name: *Apollo 11 Eagle*

Width: 4.27 metres

Height: 6.37 metres

Weight: 14.7 tonnes

Crew: Commander, pilot

Life Support: 3 days

Stages: Lower descent stage remained on Moon, upper ascent stage blasted back up into Moon orbit

Number produced: 15

Number landed on Moon: 6

The *Apollo* Lunar Module **Lander**, *Eagle*, separated from the main spacecraft. It took the astronauts to the Moon's surface before linking up with the rest of the craft again.

antenna to Earth

TV camera

antenna for Lunar Module

Three Apollo missions took lunar rovers (moon buggies).

THAT'S INCREDIBLE

The Moon has no air, water or weather. So the astronauts' bootprints in the dust will remain there for thousands of years.

New horizons

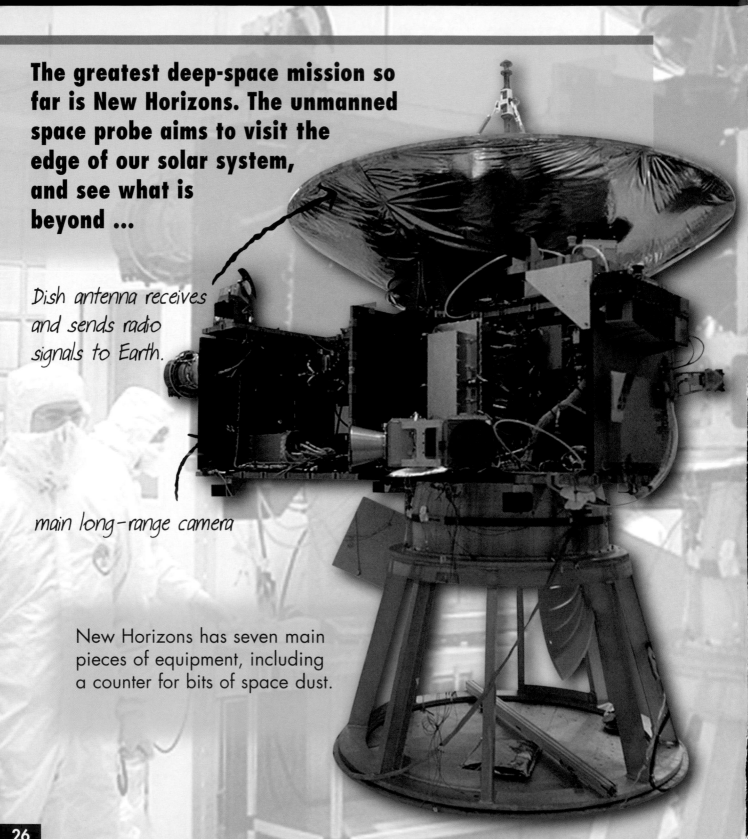

The greatest deep-space mission so far is New Horizons. The unmanned space probe aims to visit the edge of our solar system, and see what is beyond ...

Dish antenna receives and sends radio signals to Earth.

main long-range camera

New Horizons has seven main pieces of equipment, including a counter for bits of space dust.

THAT'S INCREDIBLE

A radio signal from the Moon takes less than two seconds to reach Earth. When New Horizons reaches Pluto, at the edge of our solar system, its signals will take over four hours.

Stats and Facts

New Horizons

Operator: NASA (USA)

Length: 2.7 metres

Width: 2.1 metres

Height: 2.2 metres

Weight: 478 kilograms

Launch date: 19 January 2006

Pluto flyby: 14 July 2015

Nearest approach to Pluto: 11,000 km

Nearest approach to Pluto's moon, Charon: 27,000 km

In February 2007, New Horizons flew within 2.3 million kilometres of the biggest planet, Jupiter, with its moon Io, in the foreground.

New Horizons took off on an Atlas V rocket at Kennedy Space Centre, USA.

Glossary

Antenna

An aerial for receiving and/or sending signals, usually radio or microwave signals. It may be a length of wire or shaped like a rod, dish or net.

Atmosphere

The blanket-like layer of air (mixture of gases) around Earth, which becomes thinner with height and fades to nothing in space.

Booster

A simple, powerful rocket that gives extra thrust and speed for a short time.

Comsat

A communications satellite, which receives information as radio waves or microwaves from one part of Earth, and sends it back down to another part.

Dock

In space, to join with another craft, usually with an airtight seal so that people and objects can pass from one to the other.

Gravity

The pulling force with which all objects attract each other. It gets greater with size, so Earth has huge gravity, while the Moon's is weaker.

Lander

A craft or vehicle that goes down to the surface of a space object like a planet, moon, comet or asteroid.

Laser beam

A powerful light source.

Launch vehicle

A rocket-powered craft that goes from Earth's surface into space, usually carrying a cargo or load of some kind, the payload.

Orbiter

A craft or vehicle that stays in orbit, such as around a planet or moon, while other parts called landers may go down to the surface.

Payload

The cargo, items or goods carried into space by a rocket or launch vehicle.

Probe

In space, a robotic long-distance exploring craft that has no crew.

Radio signal

Invisible waves of combined electrical and magnetic energy, often used for sending information around Earth and through space.

Rover

In space, a wheeled vehicle that travels across the surface of a planet or moon, either under control of an astronaut or by remote control.

Satellite

Any object that goes around another one in space, although the name usually refers to an artificial (man-made) object.

Satellite navigation (satnav)

Finding the way using signals from GPS (Global Positioning System) satellites high in space.

Solar panel

A device that creates electricity by collecting power from the Sun.

Solid fuel

Fuel for burning in a rocket or similar engine that is in the form of powder or bricks, rather than liquid.

Space station

A craft where people can stay for a long time, while they live and work in space.

Find out more

Websites

http://www.nasa.gov/audience/forkids/kidsclub/flash/index.html

The junior area of the massive website of NASA, the USA's National Aeronautics and Space Administration, which builds and operates many space missions.

http://www.esa.int/esaED/index.html

Fun interactive site of the European Space Agency with news, games and quizzes on all aspects of space, from the latest rocket launches to the story of the Universe.

http://www.kidsastronomy.com

Find out about space, the solar system, stars and galaxies, space travel and much more.

http://www.rivalquest.com/space

Loads of wonderful pictures about all aspects of space, including the space shuttle and space stations.

Books

Discovering Space (series), by Ian Graham, Franklin Watts, 2007

Making Sense of Science: *The Earth in Space,* by Peter Riley, Franklin Watts, 2008

Essential Science: Earth, Moon, Sun, by Peter Riley, Franklin Watts, 2006

Technology All Around Us: Space Exploration, by Clive Gifford, Franklin Watts, 2005

Earth And Space: Beyond The Solar System (series), by Steve Parker, Wayland, 2007

Note to parents and teachers:

Every effort has been made by the Publishers to ensure that the websites in this book are suitable for children, that they are of the highest educational value, and that they contain no inappropriate or offensive material. However, because of the nature of the Internet, it is impossible to guarantee that the contents of these sites will not be altered. We strongly advise that Internet access is supervised by a responsible adult.

Index